All creatures

All creatures

Poems for Children of All Ages

Malcolm E. Timms

To order additional copies of this book, contact:
Xlibris Corporation
0-800-644-6988
www.xlibrispublishing.co.uk
Orders@xlibrispublishing.co.uk
302466

Contents

INTRODUCTION

Poems this August have been my employment.
I've written them all for your enjoyment.

Some are happy, some are sad,
Some are good, some not too bad.

They're all about our fellow creatures.
Each one two different species features.

Some a moral may imply;
You may spot it if you try.

Some facts and figures you may find
Of interest to your enquiring mind.

Whether or not they cause a smile
I hope you find the read worthwhile.

THE FOX AND GOOSE

"If I could run fast," said the fox to the goose,
"And you were mobile, foot free and loose,
Then our lives would take on a much different hue.
We'd find ourselves active with so much to do."

"If I was free," said the goose to the fox,
"I'd fly in the air and out of this box.
I'd take to the sky and look down on you
And leave you alone with nothing to do."

"If you could fly high and take to the air
And I could run free and go anywhere
Then I'd visit the farm, take chickens galore
And scatter their feathers all over the floor."

"I'd fly to the coast, look over the sea,
Fly over to Holland, the Zuider Zee.
I'd visit Germany, Belgium and France,
And fly out to Iceland if I had the chance."

"I'd raid people's dustbins, steal bits of food,
Into gardens and allotments I'd boldly intrude.
I'd dig up their vegetables, nibble their flowers
Then I'd lie in the sunshine and slumber for hours."

"But all this is fancy for this is the rub:
We only exist on this sign of a pub."

THE KESTREL AND THE VOLE

Traffic flowing at great speed, but to that he pays no heed.
High above the motorway a kestrel searches for his prey.
By flying headlong to the breeze he hovers gracefully with great
ease.
With his keen sight he scours the ground; what tasty morsel can
be found?

Far below him in the grasses ignoring traffic as it passes
A harvest vole scurries about. He sniffs the air with his small
snout.
He sucks a stem his thirst to slake then pauses, the sweet air to
take.
Suddenly an aerial attack. Talons grab him on his back.
He's lifted high into the air. He's flown aloft, he knows not where.

But soon the kestrel comes to rest. He's brought the vole up to his
nest.
Four hungry beaks are waiting there ready to devour their share.
The adult bird with taloned feet tears the vole to strips of meat.
In this pursuit he sees no wrong. He wants to see his chicks grow
strong.

Some folks I know become upset. That poor young vole they can't
forget,
But Nature's cruel, or so they say. It's sad things must turn out
this way.
When you sit down with knife and fork to slice your lamb or beef
or pork,
Consider what it was in life: you don't have talons, you use a knife.

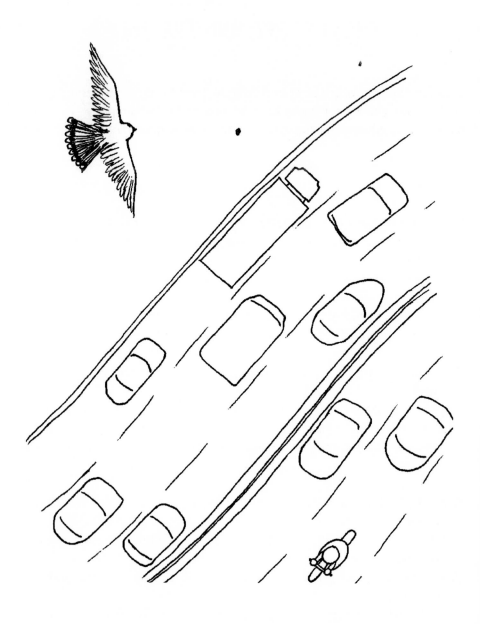

THE OWL AND THE PUSSYCAT MARK 2

The owl and the pussycat did not go to sea in a beautiful peagreen
  boat,
But they did decide to go for a ride on a very large billygoat.

The owl perched high on its horns at the front while the cat sat
  back near its tail:
"This is far more fun," they both agreed, "Than a boat on the sea
  with a sail."

The owl looked down to the ground below; the Sun was oh so
  bright.
It was half-past two in the afternoon, not two-fifteen at night.

The owl looked back and sang to the cat: "Tra-la-la-la-la!"
The cat said: "Why are you singing like that?" "I've forgotten to
  bring my guitar."

Their pennies and pounds made jingling sounds as they jogged along
  by a brook.
The five pound note inside the owl's coat was kept flat inside a small
  book.

Just after three they stopped for tea at Ronald McDonalds
  abode.
After eating their fill they settled the bill and went galloping off
  down the road.

They turned down a lane and it started to rain and the goat did not
  like it at all,
So he borrowed the cat's mobile phone and made an emergency
  call.

In the very next town was a large hotel with rooms to let for a fee;
So they made their way there, and booked separate rooms (for they were not married you see.)

They dined on pork which they ate with fork and not with a runcible spoon;
Then they had lots of fun jiving till one and didn't wake up till noon.

Then the goat submitted his bill for the ride. It was neat and written in pen,
But the owl moved away, reluctant to pay and fingered the fiver again.

"That five pound note is what I require; the fee is not so large
And if you won't pay I'll just move away and make a secondary charge."

The owl and the pussycat had no choice and gave him the five pound note.
"We were silly to ride," said the cat and he sighed. "We should have sailed away in that boat."

THE SQUIRREL AND THE WOODPECKER

For ninety years the old oak tree had slowly grown majestically.
Now it stood both tall and proud; its branches cast a mottled
    shroud.

On one high branch a squirrel stood gazing down upon the wood.
A green woodpecker he espied. It flew then settled at his side.

The squirrel looked with indignation; there had been no invitation.
"I am the owner of this tree. If your plan's to stay you must ask
    me."

"Look up there, you'll see my dray. A fine abode would you not say?
When you're around there's always a din. You're always knocking,
    but you don't move in."

"Through this tree's bark with my strong beak bugs and beetles
    there I seek
That's the noise you hear me make. I'm sorry it keeps you awake."

"Every year at autumntide I gather acorns which I hide.
A stock of food kept safe and near on which to feed throughout
    the year."

"Other birds apart from me build their nests on this fine tree.
When winter comes and it grows bitter insects hide in its leaf
    litter."

"You're right. This tree needs all our care. It's here for everyone
    to share.
It can't belong to any beast from the greatest to the least."

"For ninety years this tree has grown. It's managed that all on its
    own.
We must protect it for the nation."
"That's what I call conservation."

THE ZOO AND THE YOBS

Finding themselves with nothing to do
Three hairy yobs went to the zoo.
They first paid their money, went through the turnstile
Then stood around chatting, hung out for a while.

The elephant house was the first thing they saw
So pushing past children they went through the door.
One elephant there was bending its knees
And picking up 50p coins with great ease.

The first yob said softly: "It's time for some fun.
Let's put down just 1p and then make a run."
But the jumbo had heard him and went to its pail
And soaked him with water which made that yob wail.

From there to the parrot house the trio did go
To watch Pretty Polly and her parrot show.
One parrot was clever and rode on a skate,
But the yobs found this boring and flicked crisps at her mate.

Next to the ape house to see primate brothers:
One large male monkey, six babies, two mothers.
They flicked salted peanuts which made the apes cross,
Then the male screamed out loudly to show he was boss.

He found a large stone which he aimed without fear
And hit the lead yob on the back of his ear.
With his injured ear and damped shirt,
His trousers covered in monkey dirt,
The lead yob now was walking quite slow.
He thought to himself: "It's time we should go."

His friends, however, were not so keen.
There were so many things that they had not seen.
"We want to see the lions at least.
He really is a kingly beast."

Approaching where the lions were kept,
Their fingers ready, quite adept,
They grabbed a penguin and threw it within.
The lioness made a dreadful din:
"If you must throw chocolate bars" loudly she cursed,
"Remember to take off the wrapper first."

Now if in the future you visit a zoo;
Always remember what you should do:
Keep nuts, crisps and sweets for just your own ends
Or you're bound to end up with no animal friends.

THE PIKE AND THE STICKLEBACK

The pike is known as the freshwater shark. His mouth is full of
   teeth.
The stickleback has a spike above and another one underneath.

You may see a pike's snout in search of a trout, a fish on which he
   feeds,
But the stickleback can swim without fear in the river or among the
   reeds.

To lie quite still then make a kill, that's what a pike will like,
But the spikes of the stickle are more than a tickle in the mouth of
   the deadly pike.

If you find yourself in the mouth of a pike you'll have had it of that
   there's no doubt,
But the stickleback just wriggles about and the pike just spits him
   out.

The king of the river makes other fish quiver: the chub, the rudd,
   the dace;
But the stickleback, he has the knack, he'll meet the pike face to
   face.

Now suppose I was a river fish, what would I choose to be?
The pike is king, a terrible thing, but a stickleback, that's me.

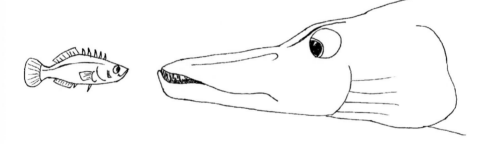

THE FROG AND THE TOAD

Said the frog to the toad: "Is beauty skin-deep?
If I had skin like yours I'd sit down and weep.

You're covered in pimples, blotches and warts.
Perhaps plastic surgery should be in your thoughts."

Said the toad to the frog: "My skin's not like yours,
But I'm still the fellow that my wife adores.

My skin will protect me from any attack.
I just exhale odours from pores on by back."

"My skin is supple, spotless and green.
I'll puff myself up, do you see what I mean?

You stand there drab with a doleful expression.
It's likely to cause you a manic depression."

Said the toad to the frog: "You're really quite crude.
Your personal comments are hurtful and rude."

Said the frog to the toad: "I feel it's my duty
To point out to you, you're hardly a beauty."

The frog's adverse comments brought pain to his head
So facing him squarely toad stood and said:

"I do not like hearing you grumble and groan
so why don't you hop it and leave me alone?"

THE SONG THRUSH AND THE SNAIL

Can you imagine the dreadful scare if someone threw your house in
the air?
If you were inside it at that time, would you think that was a
crime?

This situation is not rare for snails in gardens everywhere.
In shady places they will stay hiding from the thrush all day.

If while slithering along the ground by a song thrush he is found
Mr. Snail knows he's in trouble. His house becomes a pile of rubble.

The bird will not leave him alone. He bangs him down upon a stone.
The thrush does not seek home destruction, all he wants is food
production.

The snail may wish to make objection, but he's left with no
protection.
There's no escape, he cannot flee. The song thrush has him for his
tea.

A home is where you can reside knowing that you're safe inside:
If you live in a palace or shack you don't have to carry it on your
back.

When snails grow up they can't leave home, visit London, Paris,
Rome.
One advantage I can see, at least they get their home rent free.

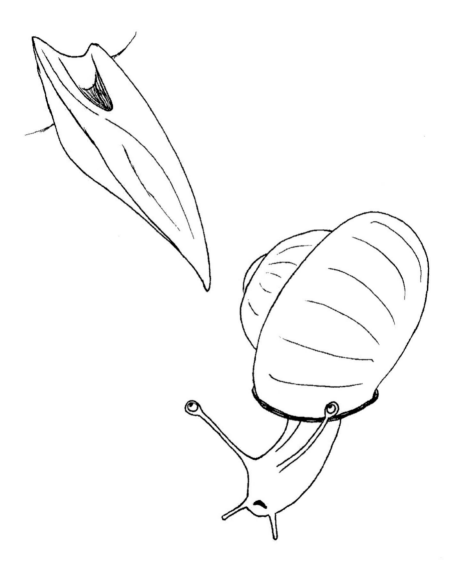

MRS.COW AND HER THREE SONS

Mrs. Cow had three young sons of whom she was quite proud.
They lived with her in cowslip field as long as she allowed.
But one fine day she called all three to find out their intent:
"What are your plans? Where will you go? I want no argument."

The first young son was bold as brass: "A fighter I shall be.
I'll go into a bullring; the crowds will cheer for me."
Now Mrs. Cow she knew just how the Spanish bulls were fought:
"In Portugal they don't kill bulls and you'll get a glass of port."

The second bull was not so brave: "A show-biz bull I'll be.
A bull to open china shops and feature on TV."
"To make a good career like that you'll need an agency.
Make sure you sign a firm contract to guarantee your fee."

The third young bull was very small, the youngest of the three.
He stood with pride at his mum's side: "What would you like to be?
Although you're small you're very fit and can travel where you
    please.
You can fly to the ends of the earth like the wind or the summer
    breeze."

"Although I'm small and very fit and could run like a zephyr.
I'd rather stay in this field always for heifer and heifer and
    heifer."

THE FLY AND THE FLEA

Said the fly to the flea: "It's quite plain to see
That human beings do not like you or me.
They hit me with papers, chase me with sprays
And try to expel me in various ways."

Said the flea to the fly: "Unlike you I can't fly
And to avoid them I just jump or hop.
Human beings, I find, are not very kind;
Their powders make me sneeze and drop."

"I can fly and annoy any man, girl or boy.
They spray me or wave me away,
But I always return, you'd think they would learn
They just can't keep me at bay."

Said the flea to the fly (and his smile was quite wry)
"As a flyer for you I'm no match,
But I think you'd agree (and he said this with glee)
I'll warrant you can't make men scratch!"

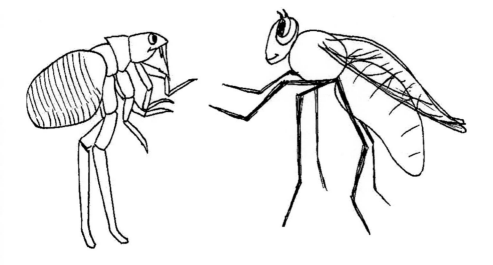

THE CAT AND THE MOUSE

"I am a cat, a very large cat.
I go out at night and hunt for a rat."

"I am a mouse, a very small mouse.
I live under the stairs in that very large house."

"To live in that house is my greatest wish
For there I would find creamy milk and fish."

"I feed on scraps that fall from the table
And steal bits of cheese whenever I'm able."

"That mouse should vanish without a trace.
Then I could move in and take his place."

"But the man in the house does not like cats
So I'll keep my place and let you hunt your rats."

THE SPIDER AND THE FLY

"Won't you come into my café?" "said the spider to the fly.
Three Ws slash arachnid will find me if you try.
We can surf the net together, find bargains by the score
Then we'll sell what we have purchased and go and buy some more."

To build a thriving business was the spider's main intent;
To make a lot of money, though his system was quite bent.
"I'll buy the goods quite cheaply then I'll sell them on once more.
We'll start to work at mid-day and finish after four."

The fly was not quite certain, he lacked a business mind
He tapped the mouse and watched the screen to see what he could
    find.
There were so many sites to see, it really was a shock.
People selling rubber tyres, a house, a single sock.

The spider watched behind the fly to see how he would do.
"You must be careful what you buy or our partnership is through!"
The fly was very canny and purchased many things
Then put them up for sale again, the phone was hot with rings.

At half-past three they both sat down their profits for to share.
"Fifty-fifty," they agreed. That surely would be fair.
But when the fly stood up to go the spider's eyes did shine.
"You're stuck upon my worldwide web! The profits all are mine."

The moral of this story I think you will agree:
Never trust a spider after half-past three.

THE HARE AND THE TORTOISE

All the animals were there to watch the tortoise and the hare:
The cat, the dog, the mouse, the horse (though he was not to run,
    of course.)

The race would be from A to B: from the alder bush to the old
    beech tree.
The weasel was to fire the gun to start the race at half-past one.

Bets were placed on who would win. Support for the tortoise was
    quite thin.
"The hare will win. It's plain to see. That tortoise could not beat a
    flea."

"The race began with great dejection: the hare had run in the wrong
    direction.
"Quick." they shouted to the hare "Run over here, not over there."

The tortoise slowly moved ahead, he paid no heed to what was
    said.
The hare ran by him at great speed then he stopped to chew a
    weed.

The tortoise kept a steady pace. He had a smile upon his face.
At four o'clock the race half-done the hare took out a currant
    bun.

"There's time enough for me to win." Then he drank a glass of gin.
He nibbled at some stalks of clover; then his legs gave way and he
    fell over.

Meanwhile the tortoise plodded on. He knew not where the hare
  had gone.
The sun beat down upon his shell. It warmed him up, he did not feel
  well.

The hare by now was feeling ill. He asked if someone had a pill.
But drink and drugs are not good news. Stay off the drugs, avoid
  the booze.

Now the beech tree was in sight. The tortoise eyes were shining
  bright.
He increased speed, ten yards an hour. That's what I call tortoise
  power.

Now he's reached the winning post. He's won the race, let's raise a
  toast.
For all who try and persevere will come out top, that is quite clear.

"But," said the tortoise "Know this well!
You'll always win if you go by shell."

THE DOG AND THE HEDGEHOG

Late one evening September,
Or was it in October? I can't remember.
Our dog went out for his relief
Then we thought he'd come to grief.

The sky was cloudy and quite dark
And then our dog began to bark.
What was the cause of his alarm?
"I must see he comes to no harm."

I took a stick and powerful torch
Then went out through our back porch.
Our dog was barking, head erect.
I did not know what to suspect.

Then I saw it near our shed.
Was it alive or was it dead?
So much noise for something small:
A baby hedgehog rolled into a ball.

For our dog this was something new.
He did not know what he should do.
To gain protection while rolled tight
A hedgehog sends out fleas which bite.

Hedgehogs now are our dog's foes
For those fleas all bit his nose.
Then they hopped from nose to ears.
I'm sure our dog then shed some tears.

The moral here then, I should say,
Go close to hedgehogs and you'll pay.
When bitten by fleas it itches and tickles
So keep your nose out of other folks' prickles.

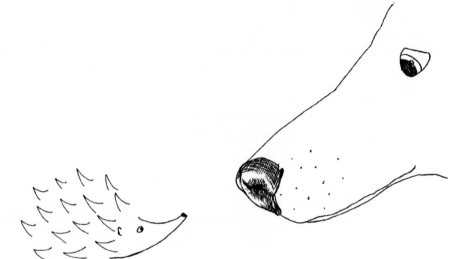

THE CUCKOO AND THE WREN

"Do you take things on deposit?" said the cuckoo to the wren.
"I'd like you to look after this until I call again."

She deposited the package among the wren's own eggs
Then flew up high and waved goodbye with her fast retreating
    legs.

The wren was rather puzzled: "What can this package Be?
The postman has already called; it is now time for tea."

Day after day the package lay immobile in its place.
The wren became quite anxious, concern was on her face.

Then tapping sounds came from within, this really was quite weird.
And then before her very eyes a baby bird appeared.

It stood up straight with opened mouth and flapped its wings quite
    wide.
It lifted all the wren's own eggs and dropped them o'er the side.

Now Jenny wren and her good mate were busy every hour
Finding food for their new guest who stayed within their bower.

It really was amazing how quickly it did grow.
Both wrens worked hard gathering food, flying to and fro.

Their guest now was enormous, the nest was rather small
And so it broke the nest apart and stood there proud and tall.

For wrens to rear a cuckoo is quite against the rules,
But wrens are canny creatures; one Wren built St. Paul's

Malcolm E. Timms

THE FLIES AND THE BEETLES

"The flies!" "The beetles!" "The fleetles!" "The bies!"
With utter confusion was heard their loud cries.
Excitement, emotion, passion, dismay,
The end of the season: cup final day.

The game was between the beetles and flies.
To win the egg cup, now that was the prize.
To train for the match the flies flew around.
The beetles went running, they stayed on the ground.

The whistle was blown at a quarter-past three.
At a quarter to four they would stop for tea.
Thirty minutes each way was thought to be wise;
Any longer was pointless for beasts of their size.

The scoring was opened by the flies' inside right.
He belted the ball with all of his mite.
By four sturdy beetles his movements were met,
But the ball ended up in the back of their net.

The beetles' first goal was at three twenty-four
And very soon after they scored seven more.
Although the flies played with much resolution
No goal could they score even with substitution.

When half-time was blown the flies were deflated
Eight-One was the score: the beetles elated
When the whistle was blown for the game to restart
The flies came out buoyant and played with new heart.

Within twenty minutes twelve eight was the score.
The beetles had eight goals, they could score no more.
Then a centipede was noticed among the flies' team.
He'd scored all their goals; he's answered their dream.

The beetles were outraged; the flies, they had cheated.
It was by this centipede they had been defeated.
"Substitutions are legal, but not recruits."
"He spent the first half tying his boots."

THE GOLDFISH AND THE HERON

Placidly swimming to and fro
In among the weeds they go,
Goldfish quite content to stay
In their pond from day to day.

Perched nearby upon a wall
A heron stands erect and tall.
"A pond." He must investigate.
A meal he can anticipate.

Unlike the osprey who's not aversed
To spy his prey then dive feet-first,
The heron always lands nearby
Then advances, feet quite dry.

He gazes down among the weed;
The goldfish prey on which he'll feed
Still are swimming unaware
Of his presence standing there.

With lightning speed a move he makes
And in his beak a fish he takes.
The other fish look for protection
Swim in fright in every direction.

He's gained his prize, he's had success;
The goldfish flaps in its distress.
He turns his head with eager eye;
To catch more fish now he must try.

When the fish stock's been depleted
Then he knows his task's completed.
With his fish he'll fly away,
But he'll return another day.

For once he's had a tasty meal
He'll think there'll be more fish to steal
And your pond he'll keep in mind
Hoping there more fish to find.

Now if you have pond with fish
And to keep them is your wish,
Around the pond some sticks you'll set
And cover over with a net.

This to a heron is interference,
They're very proud of their appearance.
No smart young heron now delights
To be seen in fishnet tights.

THE BADGER AND THE MOLE

With his head striped black and white
The badger is camouflaged when out at night.
He trundles along sniffing the air
And sometimes will dig for a mole in its lair.

The mole with its fur of velvety grey
Lives underground and just burrows away.
Every day of its life it must eat its own weight
So it eats grubs and worms at a prodigious rate.

A badger will notice a movement of ground
As a mole is burrowing without a sound.
He'll stand there and wait 'til he sees the earth rise
Then he'll dig with his claws and snatch up the prize.

Badgers are nocturnal and can see very well.
Moles are poor-sighted with a good sense of smell.
They both make their home in a hole in the earth
And it is underground to their young they give birth.

Now with all the facts that you've read in this rhyme,
Consider them carefully; just take your time,
If you had to be one of these: badger or mole,
Which one would you choose for your new life role?

THE BLACKBIRD AND THE WORM

It's mid-July, just after dawn.
A Blackbird stands upon the lawn.
With his long beak he taps the ground.
He listens for the faintest sound.

Unaware of his grave plight
A worm is burrowing out of sight.
"What's that sound I hear above?
Someone's sending a message of love."

"Could this sound be drops of rain?"
He listens: "There it is again."
The blackbird stands in expectation.
He cocks his head in his frustration.

Beneath his feet he feels a quiver.
The misty morning makes him shiver.
Wriggling upwards with great toil
The worm moves through the clammy soil.

Then with sudden pincered grab
The worm's whole body feels the stab.
He wriggles hard, but can't get free:
"I think this is the end of me.

I'm now much longer and much thinner."
The blackbird's thinking of his dinner.
The blackbird pulls with all his strength.
The worm resists it's gaining length.

A worm can turn it's often said,
But not when it is nearly dead.
But now the bird has pulled him clear
And gently whispers in his ear:

"A message of love just for you mate:
I love to have you on my plate."

THE BAT AND THE CRANE-FLY

The British bat we know so well,
(His real name is the pipistrelle)
Is nocturnal; that's to say
He wakes at night and sleeps all day.

The only mammal that can fly
When darkness falls takes to the sky.
Though almost blind, his hearing's good,
He wheels around hunting for food.

Emitting high-pitched squeaking sounds
He listens as each squeak rebounds.
This radar set is all he needs
To find the flies on which he feeds.

The daddy-longlegs (or crane-fly)
Into our homes each June will pry.
He's active both by day and night,
But has no sting and cannot bite.

It has six legs, one pair of wings
And one pair of thin stalky things.
These "halters" though very slight
Help it balance when in flight.

Any light attracts this fly
The bat knows this and so will try
To catch the crane-fly without sound
Sucked dry its shell falls to the ground.

I'll say it once and once again
Nature has her own food chain.
Each creature is food and may flourish or drop,
But humans are lucky; in the food chain we're top.

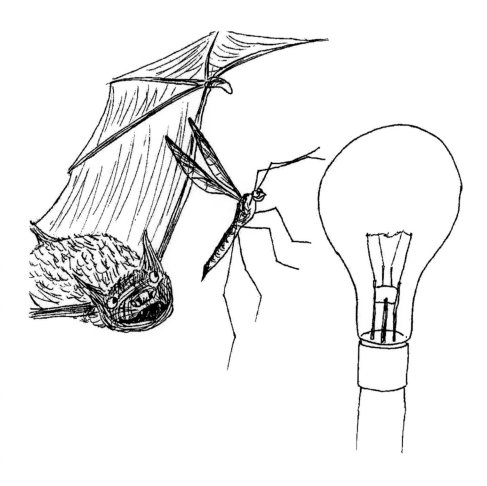

ABOUT MALCOLM

Malcolm Timms was born in Woodford Green, Essex in 1946.

On leaving school he trained for three years at Brentwood College of Education before commencing a teaching career. At college his main subject was art and craft specialising in claycraft. However, his interests extended to other arts disciplines and he became a keen member of the college drama society.

His first teaching post was at Long Ridings Junior School, where he became head of Music, and formed a school orchestra. With this orchestra he enjoyed considerable success in local and national festivals and recognition as a composer and arranger.
In 1981 he moved to John Ray Junior School, Braintree and once again formed a school orchestra. His compositions and arrangements of children's music again brought national success to his new school.

Malcolm believes that the arts disciplines inter-relate and so decided to try his hand at poetry.

He hopes they will bring amusement and pleasure to the reader. This, my second book of twenty-one poems has been illustrated as the first by Sarah Carpenter.

Lightning Source UK Ltd.
Milton Keynes UK
UKOW040436160911

178771UK00001B/104/P